BRETT FAVRE
LEADER OF THE PACK

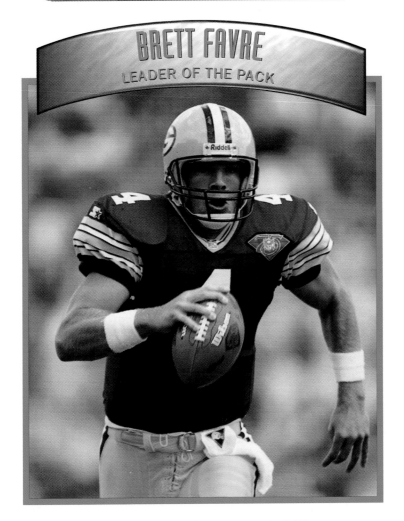

BY MARK STEWART

Children's Press®
A Division of Grolier Publishing
New York   London   Hong Kong   Sydney
Danbury, Connecticut

Photo Credits
©: Allsport USA: 22, 26 bottom, 31, 32, 39, 40 (Jonathan Daniel), 44 right (Jim Cund); AP Photo: 14 top (Morry Gash); James V. Biever: 11, 35, 36; Ron Vesely: 6, 12, 24, 26 top, 28; SportsChrome East/West: 3 (Rich Kane), 23, 25 (Ron Tringali, Jr.), 29 (Rich Kane), 43 bottom, 45 right; Tom Dipace: cover, 33, 38, 43 top, 45 left, 46; University of Southern Mississippi: 15, 17, 18, 21, 44 left.

Visit Children's Press on the Internet at:
http://publishing.grolier.com

Library of Congress Cataloging-in-Publication Data

Stewart, Mark.
    Brett Favre : leader of the pack / by Mark Stewart.
        p. cm. — (Sports stars)
        Summary: A biography of the Green Bay Packers' star quarterback who led the team to victory in Super Bowl XXXI.
    ISBN: 0-516-20969-8 (lib. bdg.)   0-516-26422-2 (pbk.)
        1. Favre, Brett—Juvenile literature. 2. Football players— United States—Biography—Juvenile literature. 3. Green Bay Packers (Football team)—Juvenile literature. [1. Favre, Brett. 2. Football players.] I. Title. II. Series.
GV939.F29S74   1998
796.332'092—dc21
[B]—dc21   97-32103
                                     CIP
                                     AC

✦ CONTENTS ✦

★ 1 ★

POISE UNDER PRESSURE

Quarterback Brett Favre cannot see the two 300-pound linemen chasing him, but he can feel them coming. Knowing he has less than two seconds to find an open teammate, he scans the field and gets ready to throw. A receiver flashes into the clear, and Brett cocks his arm. Hold it— a defensive back is laying in wait. Sensing his blockers are about to be overwhelmed, he breaks out of the pocket and narrowly avoids an oncoming pass rusher. Brett glides to the right, and the defense moves with him. One of his receivers suddenly reverses direction and gains a step on his man. That is all the room Brett needs.

He whips the ball 30 yards across the field just as he is tackled. He misses the end of the play, but he knows what happened from the explosion of cheers at Lambeau Field. The Green Bay Packers have scored a touchdown, and Brett can put another notch in his belt.

★ 2 ★

BAYOU BOY

If you ask Brett Favre to describe the place he grew up, he would probably call it "paradise." If you went there yourself, you might think he had taken too many hits to his helmet. Rotten Bayou is a snake- and alligator-infested swamp in Mississippi, the kind of place where people get lost easily. It is not too far from a major highway, and it's just a few minutes from the city of Gulfport. But it is as distant and lonely a place as you are likely to find in this country. Although Brett's hometown is listed as Kiln, the Favre home is actually in the nearby town of Fenton.

Fenton does not have a post office, or much else for that matter. In fact, the mail comes from Pass Christian, the next town over. Drive too fast and you might pass through all three towns without even knowing it!

Brett was the second of three sons born to Irvin and Bonita Favre (pronounced FARV). The three boys and their sister, Brandi, spent their days fishing, collecting crawfish, climbing trees, and getting in and out of trouble on the family's 52-acre spread. Their father was the football coach at North Hancock High School, and he also managed the local American Legion baseball team. Taught by their father, Brett, Scott, and Jeff each developed into smart and talented athletes. Brandi was also a top competitor; she starred on a number of school teams and won the title of Miss Teen Mississippi.

Brett had the strongest arm of the Favre boys. His favorite sport was football, but his best may have been baseball. He was an excellent hitter,

Brett, his father, and his two brothers pose for a photograph. Irvin Favre (second from left) gave his sons a strong athletic background.

a very good infielder, and no one wanted to face him when he took the mound. "I loved to pitch," Brett smiles. "One game, I think I struck out 15 or 16 guys, but I also hit maybe three batters right in a row. I guess some of the hitters got pretty nervous up there, but I thought that was great. It just wanted to make me throw harder."

Trained by his father from an early age, Brett has always understood the fundamentals of running a complex offense.

Brett started playing quarterback for his father in junior high school. Irvin Favre believed in running the ball and wearing the other team down; passing was not part of his game plan. Brett, however, had his own ideas. Sometimes, his father would order a running play, only to watch in shock as Brett faded back and rifled the ball to a receiver. His son was big, fast, and tough, all the qualities he liked in a player. But Brett was as stubborn as a mule when he thought he was right. That drove Coach Favre crazy. He did not like his players contradicting him, even if they were right. Even after an easy victory, Brett and his dad would sometimes yell at each other all the way to the locker room!

Brett enrolled at North Hancock High School in 1983. He did not start for the football team as a freshman, and prior to his sophomore year, he became ill with mononucleosis. To get well, Brett had to spend the next few months in bed. So instead of competing for the number-one quarterback job, he missed the season altogether.

Brett is a national sports hero, but before college, nobody knew who he was.

Now he even has his own candy bar!

Next year, Brett finally got his chance to start. Given that Irvin Favre planned to have his team run the football instead of throw it, there seemed to be little reason to pay attention to North Hancock's new quarterback. Brett says he did not mind the lack of attention. "In high school, I was no different than the quarterback at Bay High or St. Stanislaus or Pearl River Central," he recalls. "Looking back on it now, I'm kind of glad it was that way."

Brett directed the team's offense for two seasons, working hard in practice to perfect the hand-offs, pitch-outs, and fakes required to set up the various running plays. When he did throw the ball, he threw it with authority and accuracy,

Brett is still thankful for his chance to play at the University of Southern Mississippi.

but rarely was he called upon to pass more than a few times a game. When it was time to think about college, Brett found that few schools knew about him. Not a single Division-I school contacted the family. "I was never recruited for college," he says. "No one really wanted me."

Luckily, the Favre name was well-known on the campus of the University of Southern Mississippi in nearby Hattiesburg. Brett's father had been a star pitcher for the baseball team, and his brother had quarterbacked the football team. As a favor to the family, Coach Jim Carmody offered Brett a scholarship, and he accepted.

★ 3 ★

COLLEGE BALL
AND THE NFL

During preseason practice at Southern Miss, Brett tried out for quarterback and earned high praise for his intelligence, instincts, footwork, and passing arm. By the fall, he had risen to third-string on the Golden Eagle depth chart.

In the second game of the season, Southern Miss found itself trailing Tulane University at halftime, and Coach Carmody decided to put in Brett to start the second half. He probably had no intention of using Brett for more than a series or two. His idea was to shake things up and send a message to his starters. But Brett rallied his teammates around him, fired a pair of touchdown passes, and guided his team to a stirring comeback victory. The starting quarterback job was Brett's from that day on.

Brett rolls out and scans the field for an open receiver. These skills helped him flourish as a freshman starter.

Brett pitches out in a publicity shot for Southern Miss.

---- ✫ ✫ ✫ ----

Brett's four years at Southern Miss saw
him shatter more than a dozen school passing
records, despite the fact he was once again
quarterbacking a run-oriented offense. Still,
he tossed 52 touchdown passes and threw for
a total of 7,695 yards during his college career.
Brett was most highly praised, however, as
a leader. Time and again he took the Golden
Eagles from the brink of defeat to score amazing
upset victories, including a win over Florida
State that ranks as one of the most shocking
upsets of the 1980s.

Brett knew that Southern Miss had a
reputation as a second-rate football school, but
he used this as a way of whipping his teammates
into a competitive frenzy. He challenged them
to prove they were not second-rate players.
"Southern Miss was a place where everyone had
been rejected by the big schools for some reason,"
he explains. "We were the Island of Misfits.
We thrived on that. We'd play powerhouses like

Alabama and Auburn, and there would be stories about how we'd been rejected by them. We'd come out and win the game, and guys would be yelling on the field, 'What's wrong with us now?' It was a great way to play!"

As Brett completed his senior year, he had all of the qualifications of a top NFL draft choice. Pro scouts admired his skills and liked that he really seemed to be enjoying himself on the field. Football was not a job to Brett, it was still a game. The only concern about Brett was a car accident that seriously injured him two months before his senior season. His injuries required surgeons to remove 30 inches of his intestine, and they told him he might not be able to play his last year. But in the season's second game, Brett, some 30 pounds underweight, marched on to the field and stung nationally ranked Alabama 27–24. Alabama coach Gene Stallings called Brett's performance larger than life. Still, when the NFL draft was held the following spring,

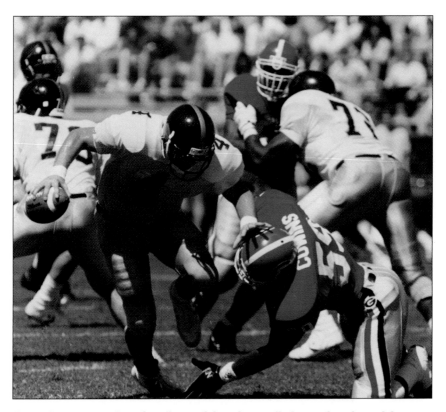

Brett's reputation for "toughing it out" dates back to his senior year, when he recovered from surgery and led his team to an 8–3 record.

it was clear that pro teams were not convinced he had fully recovered. Brett sat through the entire first round without hearing his name called. Once again, he was a football reject.

With the 33rd pick in the 1991 NFL draft, the Atlanta Falcons gambled on Brett. They were not counting on much from him, but they felt that he was worth a look. Brett made the team as the third-string quarterback and spent all but two games of his first pro

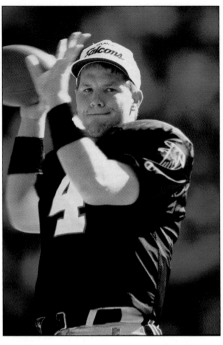

Brett practices with the Atlanta Falcons in 1991.

season sitting on the bench. Even worse, he did not get along with Atlanta coach Jerry Glanville. Brett believed he could play in the NFL, but he wondered when and where he might get a chance. He did not want to be backup forever.

In Green Bay, Wisconsin, two men were discussing this very topic. Mike Holmgren and Ron Wolf had been hired to run the Packers and to recapture the glory of the great Green Bay teams of the 1960s. As the new head coach, Holmgren planned to introduce a high-powered passing offense, similar to the one he had developed while serving as offensive coordinator for the San Francisco 49ers. As the new general manager, Wolf was in charge of stocking the team with players who could understand this

complex system. They offered a first-round draft choice for little-used Brett, and Atlanta accepted.

The new offense that Mike Holmgren has brought to Green Bay requires a quarterback like Brett who can use all of his receivers.

Brett takes over the Green Bay offense after the injury to Dan Majkowski.

Holmgren planned to ease his young quarterback into the offense. The team already had Dan Majkowski, who was called the "Majik Man" for his ability to pull games out that seemed to be lost. But against the Cincinnati Bengals in the 1992 season's third game, Majkowski went down with a knee injury and Brett was hurried into the huddle. This was exactly what the Packers hoped to avoid. But Brett rose to the occasion and threw for 289 yards and scored a dramatic 27–24 victory with time running out. Brett started for the rest of the season, leading the team to eight wins in its final 13 games. He threw for more than 3,000 yards and

It takes a bigger hit than this to knock Brett out of a game, as he has proved since his rookie year.

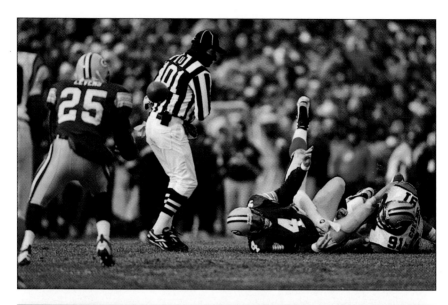

Brett's refusal to give up on plays and his willingness to pick up tough yards on his own inspires his teammates.

18 touchdowns and was named to the National Football Conference's Pro Bowl squad at season's end. More important than numbers, Brett gave the Packers what they had lacked for so many years: toughness and leadership. In a game against the heavily favored Eagles, the great defensive end Reggie White hit Brett so hard that he separated his shoulder. Brett refused to come out of the game, and he guided Green Bay to another 27–24 win.

The 1993 season began with great hope. Brett would be playing his first full year, and the defense had been improved by the signing of free-agent White, who said that he chose Green Bay over other teams because he wanted the chance to play with Brett. But all was not well with the Packers. Brett felt that the Green Bay fans expected a championship, and he began forcing plays instead of making them. Often his moves worked, but sometimes the results were disastrous. That year, he led the league in interceptions. Needless to say, Brett and Coach Holmgren argued all season long.

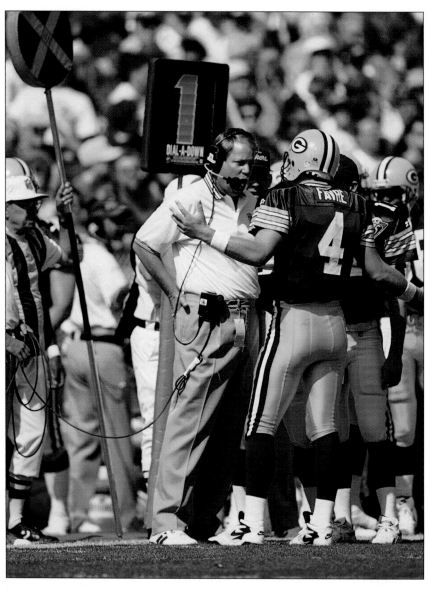

Brett and his coach often argue about how to play the game.

Brett watches a 1994 game from the sidelines with backup Mark Brunell.

Their conflict continued into the 1994 season, as Brett followed brilliant games with poor ones. In the seventh game of the season, against the Minnesota Vikings, Brett injured his hip and limped to the bench. Holmgren inserted backup quarterback Mark Brunell, who played very well. Brett was sure he had lost his starting job. The following week, most of the team's coaches urged Holmgren to go with Brunell, but he called Brett into his office and told him he would get one more shot. The coach said that Brett was very close to mastering his intricate offense, and Brett would keep his job if he showed he could do it. From that day forward, there has never been a question about who Green Bay's number-one quarterback would be. Brett wiped out the Bears 27–0 and hit 23 touchdown passes over the final nine games to take the team from 3–4 to 9–7.

Although Brett was reaching his prime as a quarterback, many believed his receivers lacked talent and experience, and this might hold him back. Sterling Sharpe, Brett's favorite receiver, suffered a career-ending neck injury in 1994. Robert Brooks was the only proven wideout on the team at the start of the 1995 season. Brett, however, had finally mastered Holmgren's system, and he had an awesome year, leading the NFL with 4,413 passing yards and 38 touchdowns. Brooks had a monster season with 102 catches, and running backs Dorsey Levens and Edgar Bennett combined for another 109.

Sterling Sharpe, Brett's favorite receiver from 1992–1994

Brett watches as Edgar Bennet bursts through the line against the Minnesota Vikings.

Mark Ingram snagged 39 passes, and tight end Mark Chmura went from 14 receptions in 1994 to 54 in 1995. When defenses dropped back and tried to clog the passing lanes, Brett handed the ball to Bennett, who piled up more than 1,000 yards. The Packers won the NFC Central Division title outright for the first time in 23 years, and Brett was named the NFL's Most Valuable Player. But a great season ended in disappointment when the Packers lost to the Dallas Cowboys in the playoffs for the third year in a row.

Brett still cannot believe that his 1995 season ended with a third-straight playoff loss to the Dallas Cowboys.

★ 4 ★

THE ULTIMATE CHALLENGE

The Cowboys were indeed a huge obstacle for Brett Favre. But then Brett experienced the biggest challenge of his life, and it had nothing to do with throwing a football. In November 1995, Brett had injured his ankle and simply played through the pain. As soon as the season ended, however, he had surgery to repair the damage. While recuperating in his hospital room, he experienced a violent seizure. As his girlfriend, Deanna, and their daughter, Brittany, watched in horror, Brett's arms, legs, and head began shaking uncontrollably. His eyes rolled back into his head and he lost consciousness for several minutes.

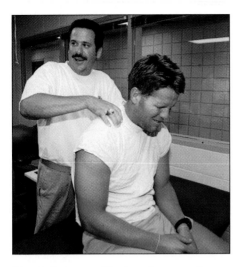

Brett knows that aches and pains are part of life in the NFL.

Brett knew what the problem was. For more than a year he had been taking a painkiller called Vicodin. The drug took away the pain from the bruises and sprains he got during games. He became so used to taking the pills that he often swallowed them when his body felt fine; when he was really hurting, he had to take a handful of pills just to get some relief. When he ran out of pills, he would ask his friends and family to get them for him. He became addicted to the drug, and for more than a year he ignored his body's warning signs. "The pills enabled me to escape the realities of being a quarterback and a star," Brett explains. The seizure, said the doctors, might be his final warning. The next time, he could die.

Brett and Deanna watch their daughter, Brittany, cut their wedding cake.

Brett checked himself into a rehabilitation program so he could clean the Vicodin out of his system and break his dependency. It was harder than he ever imagined. The doctors and therapists were tougher on him than any coach he had ever had—including his dad! But after two months Brett was clean and ready to get in shape for the 1996 campaign. He married his longtime love, Deanna, and dedicated his season to his good friend Mark Haverty, who had died in an automobile accident that year.

What a season it was! The Packers added several key role players on both sides of the football, and Brett was every bit as good as he had been in 1995. By playoff time, Green Bay had secured the all-important home-field advantage with the NFC's best record. That meant all challengers would have to come to Lambeau Field, where the Packers were practically unbeatable.

First, Brett had to get past the San Francisco 49ers. Game day was cold and rainy. The 49ers hoped Brett would try to pass his team to victory. They planned to intercept or block bad throws that the rainy weather was bound to cause. But that was the old Brett Favre. The new Brett threw only when necessary, and he let his teammates take the game to their opponents. Although he passed for just 79 yards, Brett was credited with leading his team to a 35–14 victory. "One man can't do it. It takes a team effort," he said. "I don't know if, three years ago, I would've said that, but that's what made me a better quarterback."

Brett hands off against the San Francisco 49ers in the 1996 playoffs.

The Dallas Cowboys did not play as intelligently in their game against the Carolina Panthers, and they lost. Later, a few Dallas players admitted that the Packers, not the Panthers, were on their mind. This incredible upset meant that Brett would not need to unseat the hated Cowboys to make it to the Super Bowl. But he would have to face his old backup, Mark Brunell, who was now Carolina's starter.

Brett barks out signals during the 1996 NFC Championship Game against the Carolina Panthers.

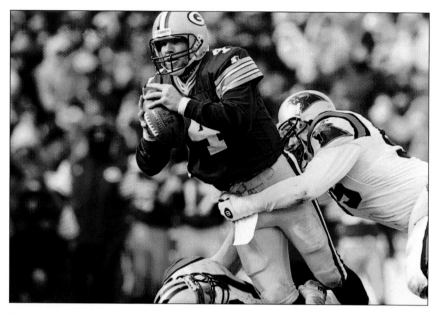

Brett struggles to get rid of the ball against the Panthers in the 1996 title game.

In the opening quarter, Brett made a bad pass that was intercepted deep in Green Bay territory. Carolina linebacker Lamar Lathom got in Brett's face after the interception and warned him that it was going to be a long day. Brett shrugged and said, "We'll see." It turned out to be a long day for the Panthers. Brett handled himself beautifully, and the defense kept the pesky Brunell at bay in an easy 30–13 win. The Packers were on their way to the Super Bowl for the first time in 29 years.

★ 5 ★

SIMPLY SUPER

The two weeks prior to Super Bowl XXXI seemed like an eternity to Brett Favre. Their opponents, the New England Patriots, were the surprise champs of the AFC. Brett had studied all the films, practiced all the plays, and attended all the game meetings he cared to. All he wanted to do was play. Then, the night before the big game, Brett got sick. He felt weak and his temperature hovered above 101 degrees. "I was worried," he admits. "I'd waited my whole life to play this game, and now I wasn't healthy."

As always, Brett simply toughed it out. Early in the game, he noticed a weakness in New England's defensive plan and called a new play right at the line of scrimmage. Just as he had hoped, wide receiver Andre Rison broke into the clear, and Brett hit him with a perfect spiral for a 54-yard score.

The Pats hung tough and took a 14–10 lead. Again, Brett spotted a weakness in the defense and called a new play. This time, he threw a strike to receiver Antonio Freeman, who scampered the length of the field for an 81-yard touchdown. Later, as he stood on the sideline, Brett realized that he probably would not have called these plays just a couple of seasons earlier. As badly as he had wanted to reach the Super Bowl all those years, he had come to this game at just the right time in his career. The game ended with a Green Bay victory.

With one NFL championship under his belt, Brett dedicated himself to being the best player he could be—perhaps the best player ever. In 1997–98, he earned his third NFL Most Valuable Player award and led the Packers back to the Super Bowl. The 1998 Super Bowl was a thrilling and hard-fought contest. In the final two minutes, the under-dog Denver Broncos scored the go-ahead touchdown and won the game. Brett was disappointed, but he learned a valuable lesson. No matter how confident and talented he is, he will always work harder to improve his game.

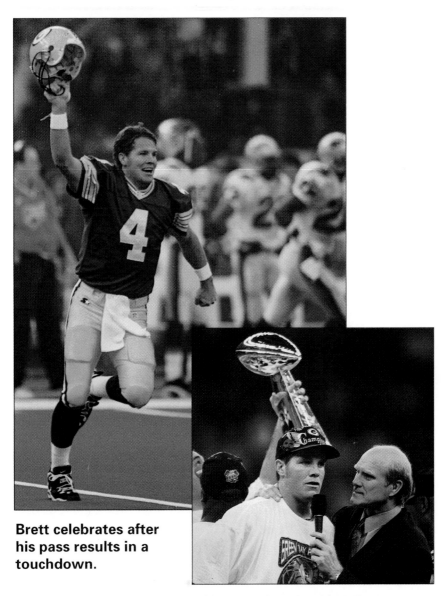

Brett celebrates after his pass results in a touchdown.

After winning the 1997 Super Bowl, Brett speaks with Hall-of-Famer Terry Bradshaw.

C ⋆ H ⋆ R ⋆ O ⋆ N

1969 • October 10: Brett is born in Gulfport, Mississippi.

1987 • Brett receives a scholarship to play at Southern Mississippi University. He becomes the starting quarterback.

1991 • Atlanta Falcons select Brett in the second round of the NFL draft.

1992 • Atlanta Falcons trade Brett to the Green Bay Packers.

• After Dan Majkowski is injured, Brett becomes the starting quarterback. He finishes the season with 3,000 yards in passing and is named to the NFC's Pro Bowl squad.

1994 • Brett again produces a Pro Bowl season, but the Packers lose to the Dallas Cowboys in the playoffs.

O ⋆ L ⋆ O ⋆ G ⋆ Y

1995 • Brett leads the Packers to the NFC Central Division title and is named the NFL's Most Valuable Player.

1996 • Brett experiences a violent seizure. Admitting his dependence on Vicodin, a pain-killing drug, Brett enters a rehabilitation program.

• Brett completes the rehabilitation program. He leads the Green Bay Packers through the playoffs to a Super Bowl win over the New England Patriots.

1997 • Brett leads the Packers back to the Super Bowl and wins his third NFL Most Valuable Player award. The Packers, however, lose to the Denver Broncos.

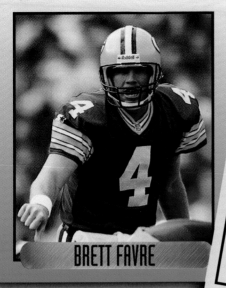

BRETT FAVRE

BRETT FAVRE

Name **Brett Lorenzo Favre**

Born **October 10, 1969**

Place of Birth **Gulfport, MS**

Height **6' 2"**

Weight **225 pounds**

Home **Diamondhead, MS**

NFL's Most Valuable Player **1995, 1996, & 1997**

Super Bowl Champion **1997**

NFL STATISTICS

Year	Att	Comp	Pct	Yards	TDs
1991	5	0	0.0	0	0
1992	471	302	64.1	3,227	18
1993	522	318	60.9	3,303	19
1994	582	363	62.4	3,882	33
1995	570	359	63.0	4,413*	38*
1996	543	325	59.9	3,899	39*
1997	513	304	59.3	3,867	35
Total	3206	1971	61.5	22,591	182

* Led NFL

--- ✯ ✯ ✯ ---

ABOUT THE AUTHOR

Mark Stewart grew up in New York City in
the 1960s and 1970s—when the Mets, Jets, and
Knicks all had championship teams. As a child,
Mark read everything about sports he could lay
his hands on. Today, he is one of the busiest
sportswriters around. Since 1990, he has written
close to 500 sports stories for kids, including
profiles on more than 200 athletes, past and
present. A graduate of Duke University, Mark
served as senior editor of *Racquet,* a national
tennis magazine, and was managing editor
of *Super News*, a sporting goods industry
newspaper. He is the author of every Grolier
All-Pro Biography and eight titles in the
Children's Press Sports Stars series.

jB
FA

Stewart, Mark.

Brett Favre.

MAR   1999